Ceremonies and Celebrations

PILGRIMAGES AND JOURNEYS

SUE KENDALL

RSVP RAINTREE
STECK-VAUGHN
PUBLISHERS

A Harcourt Company

Austin   New York
www.steck-vaughn.com

Ceremonies and Celebrations

PILGRIMAGES AND JOURNEYS

Other titles in this series are:

BIRTHS • WEDDINGS • GROWING UP
LIFE'S END • FEASTS AND FASTING

Published by Raintree Steck-Vaughn Publishers, an imprint of Steck-Vaughn Company

Library of Congress Cataloging-in-Publication Data is available upon request.

ISBN 0-7398-3271-9

Printed in Italy. Bound in the United States.
1 2 3 4 5 6 7 8 9 0 05 04 03 02 01

Picture acknowledgments
Circa Picture Library 13, 17 (Robyn Beeche); Hutchison Library 5 (J. Horner), 8 (B. Regent), 25; Peter Sanders 19, 20, 21; Tony Stone Images front cover bottom left (Nabeel Turner), 6 (Louis Grandadam), 10 (Paul Chesley), 16 (David Sutherland); Trip front cover top left (Dinodia), front cover top right (H. Rogers), front cover bottom right (F. Good), 1 (A. Tovy), 4, 7 (M. Both), 9 (Z. Harasym), 11 (H. Isachar), 12 (A. Tovy), 14 (Dinodia), 15 (Resource Foto), 18, 22 (Dinodia), 23 (J. Sweeney), 24 (H. Rogers), 26 (H. Rogers), 27 (H. Rogers), 28 (H. Rogers), 29 (H. Rogers).

CONTENTS

What is a Pilgrimage?

People all over the world have places that are very special for them. Sometimes these are places that remind them of a particular person or event, and sometimes they are places that help them remember why they joined the religion that they follow, thereby strengthening their faith.

Millions of Muslims visit Mecca every year to make the Hajj *pilgrimage.* ▼

People often choose to travel to these sites because it is part of their religious tradition. Often with other followers, they journey to places of religious significance, such as shrines or holy cities.

This type of visit is sometimes called a pilgrimage. Pilgrimages can be made alone or with a few friends and family, but often a large group of believers will go on a pilgrimage together. In some faiths a pilgrimage may be a once in a lifetime event, while for others it may happen every year or even more regularly than that.

A special journey

When pilgrims arrive at the place of pilgrimage, they often perform rituals and worship together. For many, part of the pleasure of a pilgrimage is being with people who have the same beliefs as themselves. Other people may choose to pray or meditate quietly on their own. A pilgrimage is a special time, and many pilgrims spend years saving up and preparing for pilgrimages to faraway places.

This book will introduce you to pilgrimages from the six main world religions. It will tell you about some of the journeys and pilgrimages that believers go on.

▲ *Pilgrimages can be quiet times, when a pilgrim can pray privately to God. This Jewish man is praying at the Western Wall, all that remains of Solomon's Temple in Jerusalem.*

The Christian Tradition

There are lots of places, all over the world, where Christians choose to go on a pilgrimage. Christians believe that God sent his son, Jesus, from heaven to Earth to teach people how to live good lives. While Jesus was on Earth he preached God's word to people. Many Christians go to visit places that were important in Jesus' life on Earth. Others go to places where they believe miracles have happened.

Christians go on pilgrimages for many reasons: to renew their faith, to seek a cure for illness, to thank God for something good, or to ask God's forgiveness if they have done something wrong. Pilgrimages can take place at any time, but many Christians choose to go at festival times or on the anniversary of a special event. Many believers find that being with other pilgrims helps strengthen their faith.

▲ At special times, such as Easter, the Pope, the Bishop of Rome, blesses crowds of pilgrims in open-air services outside Saint Peter's Basilica in Rome's Vatican City.

Rome–The Holy City

Some Christians choose to visit places that have been important in the history of Christianity. Many people make the journey to Rome, Italy, the center of the Roman Catholic Church. Two of Christ's apostles, Saint Peter and Saint Paul were martyred in Rome. The Catacombs and the Colisseum are other places of pilgrimage associated with early Christianity.

Sophie's story

"My name is Sophie. Last Easter I went with my mother on a pilgrimage to Jerusalem to see where Jesus died and rose again. It was quite warm when we got there. We went to the old city where there were thousands of people all walking very slowly behind men carrying a heavy wooden cross—just like Jesus did on his own. As we followed behind, people were praying quietly to themselves or joining in hymns. It made me feel very special to know that this is where Jesus had walked."

▲ *Pilgrims follow the path that Christ took to his crucifixion during this procession along the Via Dolorosa in Jerusalem on Good Friday.*

The Holy Land

At some time in their lives, many Christians travel to the Holy Land, where Jesus lived about 2,000 years ago. They can visit Bethlehem where he was born, Nazareth where he grew up, and Galilee, where he told people about God's teachings. In Jerusalem, Christians can follow the route of Jesus' entry into the city on Palm Sunday. On Good Friday he was led down the Via Dolorosa to his crucifixion. The ancient Romans, who ruled over Israel, crucified Jesus. Pilgrims can see the tomb from which Jesus rose on Easter Day.

Easter is especially important for Christians and many visit Jerusalem during this time. Many pilgrims join the procession along the Via Dolorosa and relive the events of Good Friday, when Jesus was crucified. They pray and think about how Jesus gave his life for them.

▲ *Pilgrims join a healing ceremony at Lourdes, France, hoping to be cured of their illnesses.*

Shrines and Miracles

All over the world there are sites where the saints lived or where miracles have taken place. There are also places, such as Fatima in Portugal or Guadalupe in Mexico, where the Virgin Mary is said to have appeared. Very often people go to these shrines to pray for people who are ill or suffering and to ask God to cure them. Many people make the journey to Lourdes in France.

Christians believe the Virgin Mary appeared here in 1858 to a young girl and showed her a source of healing water. When they come to Lourdes, many Christians join in healing services, or pray quietly. Others choose to collect holy water to take home, because they believe that it will bring them good health and blessings.

Worshipers in Poland carry a statue of the Virgin Mary. Polish Catholics believe that the Virgin has aided their country many times in the past. Frequently they visit shrines that honor her. ▼

Sacred text

This text tells of Jesus and his family going on a pilgrimage to Jerusalem for Passover, and how the boy Jesus stayed behind to talk to wise men to increase his knowledge of the scriptures.

"Now his parents went to Jerusalem every year at the feast of the Passover. And when he was twelve years old, they went up to Jerusalem after the custom of the feast. And when they had fulfilled the days, as they returned, the child Jesus tarried [stayed] behind in Jerusalem and Joseph [Jesus' father] and his mother knew not of it. And it came to pass, that after three days they found him in the temple, sitting in the midst of the doctors, both hearing them and asking them questions."

The Bible: Luke 2:41-47

The Jewish Tradition

Jews believe that more than 3,000 years ago, God rescued their ancestors, who were slaves in Egypt. He chose Moses to lead them to the "Promised Land," the area of modern Israel, although at that time it was called Canaan. During the last century many Jews returned to that area and established the State of Israel. Jews believe that God gave them the Promised Land because they are his chosen people. Many Jews from different parts of the world like to visit Israel to remember the great events of their history.

This Jewish man is praying in front of the Western Wall. He is carrying a Jewish prayer book. ▼

The Western Wall

There are lots of special places in the land of Israel, that believers like to visit. Jerusalem is the ancient city that is at the heart of the religion. When they visit the city, most Jewish people like to take time to go and pray at the Western Wall. This is the last remaining part of the famous Jewish Temple, that was destroyed in A.D. 70. Many worshipers gather at the Western Wall to recite the ancient traditional prayers. Men and women pray separately and some cry as they remember the history of the Jewish people. Some write special prayers on small pieces of paper and push these into the cracks between the stones of the ancient temple, hoping that their prayers will be answered.

Sacred text

This is an extract from the prayer that Jews say before going on a journey.

"May it be thy will, O Lord our God and God of our fathers, to conduct us in peace unto the haven of our desire. O deliver us from every enemy, ambush and hurt by the way, and from all afflictions that visit and trouble the world."

From the Authorized Daily Prayer Book

Many years ago, every Jew was expected to go to the ruins of the Temple for Pesach (Passover), Shavuot, and Sukkot; these festivals are known as the Pilgrim Festivals. Nowadays there are no fixed times when Jews should make pilgrimages, but many choose to go during the main festivals and holidays, when they can join in holiday fun with family and friends. Hasidic Jews, who follow the traditional form of Judaism, may make pilgrimages to the graves of their leaders or respected Jewish scholars.

The Holocaust

Some Jewish people also choose to make a special journey to Yad Vashem. This is the place where a memorial has been built to remember all the Jewish people who were killed or suffered during the Holocaust last century. When they visit, some people say traditional prayers or light candles. Others cry as they think about what happened. Some just listen to a tape that gives the names of all the children who died in the death camps of Europe. The camps were set up by the Nazis during World War II to destroy the Jewish people.

◀ *This memorial at Yad Vashem in Jerusalem shows Jewish men, women, and children fighting against Nazi soldiers during World War II.*

The kibbutz

Many of the ancient places that Jews choose to visit in Israel help them remember their history. With the aim of building a stronger future for the Jewish people, Jews today often travel to a kibbutz. It has become popular for young Jewish adults to go to Israel to live and work on a kibbutz—giving up their spare time to deepen their understanding of what it means to be a Jew and learning to live as part of a community. Here they work and live together, practice their faith, and try to do something to help the State of Israel. Duties include working on the land and helping with community projects.

This Jewish woman is gathering fruit as part of her daily duties as a kibbutz member. ▼

The ceremonial Seder plate contains symbolic foods: bitter herbs, vegetables, bitter vegetables, an apple, nut, spice and wine mixture (Charoset), a shank bone (leg bone) of whatever meat the family is eating, and an egg.

Passover

Even if they cannot go to Israel, many Jews around the world celebrate a special festival called Pesach, or Passover. This reminds them of a very special journey that the ancient Israelites had to make to escape the persecution of the Egyptians. They celebrate by sharing a *Seder* meal together. They use symbolic foods and drink to remind them how God looked after them. They also read the story of that journey in the Bible, play games, and enjoy time together as a family.

Ben's story

"My name is Ben and I am 12. I live in New York City with my mom and dad and three sisters. Last year our family traveled to Israel. I felt very honored that I could go the Western Wall with dad. We said our prayers side by side, and I even wrote a prayer for my sick grandma and stuck it in the wall itself. Going to Israel helped me remember our history and made me proud to be Jewish. One day I'd like to come back again!"

The Hindu Tradition

In the Hindu religion people go on many different pilgrimages and journeys. Some Hindus consider it a duty to go on a pilgrimage, or *Yatra*, as it earns special merit with the gods, good fortune, health and happiness. If they choose to make a pilgrimage, it is often to a place that has a special meaning for their chosen deity, such as Krishna or Vishnu. Different Hindu families worship different deities (gods), who are all various aspects of Brahman, the One True Spirit. There are lots of legends and stories about the lives of the deities, and some believers like to visit places where these stories took place.

These Hindus are on an annual pilgrimage to Puri, Orissa, where Lord Krishna's bones are said to have been taken when he died. ▼

▲ *This couple, in Varanasi, are taking part in a performance of the* Ramayana *story. They are dressed as the gods Rama and Sita.*

Places of pilgrimage

There are hundreds of different places that Hindus might go and visit, but there are four very famous places of pilgrimage; Varanasi, where the wonderful *Ramayana* story (the Hindu epic poem about Prince Rama) is acted out for all the worshipers to see; Vrindaban, which many believe was the birthplace of Lord Krishna; Rameshwaram, where the God Rama is said to have worshiped Shiva to ask forgiveness for killing someone, and Puri in Orissa, sacred to Lord Krishna (Vishnu), where many Hindus enjoy joining in as a giant statue of the God in a huge chariot is pulled through the town.

Sacred text ॐ

This text tells Hindus that they should read the sacred texts and show their devotion to God by doing godly things—such as going on pilgrimages. "Austerity, the study of sacred texts and the dedication of action to God constitute the discipline of mystic union."

From the *Yoga Sutra* of Patanjali

Holy rivers

Hindus have a great respect for the natural environment and often make pilgrimages to important rivers and water sources, such as the Ganges, Kaveri, and Indus rivers. Many Hindu people try to visit the Ganges River in India. Bathing in its holy waters symbolizes that they are trying to lead pure and clean lives. Many confess their sins at the river. The journey is part of the pilgrimage, and some Hindus will make the traveling as difficult as they can. Some may choose to walk or crawl part of the way because they believe this proves their devotion and will find them favor with the gods.

Hindus believe in life after death. They accept that everyone is reborn in a different form, either a higher or lower life form. Because of this, they believe in cremation after death. They are taught that the fire releases the human spirit to be reborn into another life. After the cremation, Hindus will often scatter the ashes of their loved one into a river, because it is a holy place.

Bathers come to Varanasi from all over India, to bathe in the holy waters of the Ganges River. This picture shows the Dasaswamedh Ghat (steps). ▼

Holidays and worship

Ashvin's story

"I am Ashvin and I am just about to turn 11. I live in New York City with my parents, two sisters, and my grandmother. Last year my grandad died and we were all very sad. After he was cremated we all flew to India. We made the journey to the holy Ganges River at Varanasi, where we all bathed to make ourselves clean and pure. Later my dad scattered grandad's ashes over the water."

Whichever site they visit, Hindus meditate and worship the gods. Sometimes they will join in singing, chanting, and dancing together. Many Hindus also make offerings and light candles to show devotion to God. *Yatra* is a happy and joyful time when believers meet other Hindus and listen to the teachings of the priests. Sometimes a pilgrimage gives them the chance to visit new places, have a vacation, and catch up with old friends and family members. Many choose to make a pilgrimage at a time when something important, such as a wedding or birth, is going to happen to them. They believe it brings good luck.

Pilgrims, covered in dyes that are traditionally thrown at the festival of Holi, follow the pilgrimage route at Vrindaban. Here they visit the place where they believe that Krishna was born. ▶

The Muslim Tradition

For many Muslims, the greatest way to strengthen their faith and show devotion to Allah, the One God, is a pilgrimage to the holy city of Mecca. Muslims believe it was here that the Prophet Muhammad received the Word of God and was instructed to teach Muslims how to lead a good life.

The Hajj pilgrimage

Muslims try to lead a sin-free life and fulfill their duties. One of these duties, the fifth of the Five Pillars of Islam (the laws that Muslims should follow), is to try to go on the *Hajj* pilgrimage at least once during their lifetime. Muslims go to Mecca because they believe it was there that the Prophet Abraham built the *Ka'bah*, the monument to One God. The Koran calls all Muslims to pilgrimage there.

Muslim women gather at the harem (women's quarters) at the start of the Hajj *pilgrimage.* ▼

▲ *Muslims circle the Ka'bah. They believe that it contains the stone that God threw at Adam when he expelled him from Paradise for disobeying him.*

Every year, millions of Muslims from all over the world go on the *Hajj*. People who are sick or who cannot go may pay for someone else to go in their place.

The *Hajj* always takes place betwen the 8th and 13th day of the Islamic month of Dual-Hijah. Only Muslims are allowed into Mecca at any time. *Hajj* is an exciting time, but also very tiring. It is a time when all Muslims show that they are equal before God and men try to dress in the *Ihram*—simple white clothes made from two seamless pieces of cloth. These clothes represent purity, chastity, and equality. Women can wear any respectable clothes.

Sacred text

This sacred text tells how God commanded Abraham to call men to *Hajj* at Mecca.

"And proclaim unto mankind the pilgrimage. They will come unto thee on foot and on every lean camel; they will come from every deep ravine."

Koran: XXII 27

Rituals of Hajj

▲ *A Muslim woman drinks from the* Well of Zamzam.

Muslims show that they are all the same by performing the same rituals and actions of *Hajj* together. Many *Hajj* rituals recall the experiences of the Prophet Abraham, his wife, Hagar, and their son, Ishmael. *Hajjis* walk in Abraham's family's footsteps when they are there, as a way of remembering their devotion to God.

Everybody circles the *Ka'bah* (a black stone structure that all Muslims must turn toward when they pray) seven times, kissing the stone, pointing at it or touching it as they start each circuit. Next the *Hajjis* (pilgrims) run between the two hills of Safa and Marwa as Hagar, Abraham's wife, did in search of water. As they walk or run, they drink from the *Well of Zamzam* where water miraculously appeared to quench Hagar's thirst. On the 9th day of the month, they travel to Mount Arafat where the Prophet Muhammad gave his last sermon. While here they say prayers and confess their sins. Then they travel to Muzdalifah to camp for the evening.

Here they say prayers again and read the Koran throughout the night. The next morning the *Hajjis* gather stones that they take to throw at the three pillars at Jamarat. These pillars represent Satan (the devil). On the tenth day the *Hajjis* join together for the feast of *Al Adha*. This helps them remember that Abraham was prepared to kill his son for his faith, but instead God told him to sacrifice a ram. Near the end of the pilgrimage, everyone circles the *Ka'bah* once more before changing back into ordinary clothes to travel home.

Muslims consider it a special honor to be able to join the *Hajj*. Millions of pilgrims arrive for *Hajj* from all over the world by plane and boat. Many have to save money to make the journey. They go not only because it is their duty, but also because it helps them strengthen their faith.

Danah's story

"I am Danah and I'm 11 years old! I share a house with my parents and older brother. This year was very exciting because my brother and dad went on *Hajj* to Mecca. They told me that they would say special prayers for me and mother in Mecca. They brought us some holy water from the *Well of Zamzam*. Dad has carefully folded the clothes he wore on *Hajj*, and says he wants to keep them forever. He also wants to make sure he is buried in them."

◀ Hajjis *throw stones at the pillars of Jamarat.*

The Buddhist Tradition

Buddhists try to follow the teachings of the Buddha. He was a very wise teacher who lived in Nepal around 560 B.C. He was born a wealthy prince, but left his luxurious lifestyle behind to find out the reasons for suffering and evil. He spent many years trying to find the answers. He eventually understood what causes suffering and how to escape from it and became the Buddha —an Enlightened being. The Buddha taught people how to live so that they could free themselves from suffering and gain Enlightenment. He taught them to follow the Eightfold Path. All Buddhists should try to develop:

▲ This picture shows the Buddha sitting under a Bodhi tree in Bodh Gaya, where he became Enlightened.

- Right Views, by understanding that all things change and so develop wisdom.
- Right Intention (thoughts), by committing themselves to grow and change for the better.
- Right Speech, by telling the truth and speaking in a kind and friendly way.
- Right Action, by trying not to harm living beings (steal from, kill or hurt other people or animals).
- Right Livelihood, by doing work that doesn't harm oneself or others.
- Right Effort, by trying to develop an attitude of kindness and generosity to all (following the Eightfold Path with kindness).
- Right Mindfulness, by being aware of themselves, other people and the world around them.
- Right Concentration, by training the mind in meditation to be calm and positive in order to develop wisdom.

◀ *Pilgrims decorate the Bodhi tree that they believe Buddha sat underneath.*

The journey of life

During their lives, Buddhists try to follow this pathway and many think of it as a journey that they are on, even though they are not going to a different place! Some people may try to go and visit important places in Buddhist history. The four most popular sites are Lumbini (Nepal), where they believe Siddartha Gautama, the man who became the Buddha, was born; Bodh Gaya (India), where he achieved Nirvana or Enlightenment; Sarnath (India), where he gave his first teaching, and Kushinagar (India), where he died. Pilgrims believe that visiting these special places where they believe the Buddha lived and taught helps them in their practice of Buddhism.

Sacred text

In this text, the Buddha tells his disciple, Ananda, about pilgrimages.

"Ananda, there are four places the sight of which should arouse emotion in the faithful. Which are they? 'Here the Tathagata (Buddha) was born,' is the first [Lumbini]. 'Here the Tathagata attained supreme Enlightenment' is the second [Bodh Gaya]. 'Here the Tathagata set in motion the Wheel of Dhamma' [where he gave his teachings] is the third [Sarnath]. 'Here the Tathagata attained the Nibbana-element [total peace] without remainder' is the fourth [Kushinagar, where he died]. And Ananda, the faithful monks and nuns, male and female lay followers will visit those places."

Digha Nikaya: *Maha Parinibbana Sutta*

Temples and sacred buildings

Sometimes followers cannot make the long journeys to these places, so they visit temples and *stupas* (sacred monuments) nearer to their homes. Wherever they choose to visit, they pay their respects to the Buddha. Many will listen to the teachings of the monks, join in chanting, and make offerings of flowers, gifts, and incense. They may help redecorate the statue of the Buddha or meditate quietly under a nearby tree—just as the Buddha once did. All these activities help them concentrate on their own journey of life, following the Eightfold Path.

These monks are praying in a park at Sarnath, where the Buddha gave his first teachings. ▼

Wesak

There is no particular time when Buddhists go on a pilgrimage, but it is good to go during a Buddhist festival when they can meet lots of other Buddhists. Visiting holy places with other members of the Buddhist *sangha* (community) helps them think about the Buddha and strengthens their resolve to follow his teachings more deeply. Lots of Buddhists like to visit special places at *Wesak*. *Wesak* is the main Buddhist festival. It is celebrated by Buddhists during the full moon in May and June. It recalls the life, birth, and Enlightenment of the Buddha. The pilgrimage sites are usually specially decorated at this time.

It is not only practicing Buddhists who visit shrines and special places. Often people from other religions and traditions also like to make the same journeys. They find it helpful and restful to listen to the wise teachings from the monks and to meet and talk with the Buddhists.

Ian's story

"My name is Ian. I live with my mother and father in Holland. We are Buddhists and often go to the local temple to meet friends. Recently a group of us went to Lumbini, where the Buddha was born. There were so many people walking up the hill to the monastery. When we got there we listened to the monks' teaching and wise words. The statues of the Buddha were so beautiful and I enjoyed helping to decorate one of them. I put a large bunch of bright flowers at the Buddha's feet."

This stupa is in Sarnath. Here pilgrims visit the shrine to the Buddha and remember the Buddha's teachings. ▶

The Sikh Tradition

The Sikh religion started in the Punjab just over 500 years ago, when Guru Nanak received a calling (he was spoken to by God) to lead his people and teach them how to follow God. The teachings do not say that believers have to go on pilgrimages to special places, but many Sikhs like to go back to the Punjab in northern India and see where the *Gurus* lived and taught. Many of them think of it as a way of showing that they are Sikhs and of strengthening their faith.

The Golden Temple

Guru Nanak was the first of the ten *Gurus*. Many of the special sites that Sikhs choose to visit are places where important events happened in the lives of the *Gurus*. Some Sikhs like to visit the Golden Temple at Amritsar because it is one of the most important sites in the religion.

The Golden Temple at Amritsar is seen as a symbol of the strength and magnificence of Sikhs all over the world. ▼

▲ *Children enjoy ritual bathing in the lake at the Golden Temple, Amritsar, India.*

Sacred text

This text from the Sikh holy book talks about how Sikhs should devote themselves to God.

"The souls on their spiritual journey chant and meditate within their minds on the One Lord, the Treasure of Excellence. The Righteous judge of Dharma serves them; blessed is the Lord who adorns them."

From the *Guru Granth Sahib*

The fifth *Guru*, Arjan Dev, built this beautiful temple. It stands in a lake, and in order to enter you have to step down into the building. This shows that you are being humble as you enter this special place. The temple has four entrances, each facing a different direction. This shows that Sikhs welcome everybody, from all parts of the world and that they are all equal. The belief in equality is important to Sikhs.

▲ *Worshipers share the* langar *meal from leaf plates in the Golden Temple at Amritsar. This meal symbolizes the equality of all Sikhs.*

Sikh worship

When believers go into the Golden Temple, they listen to the *Guru Granth Sahib*, the holy book, being recited by the *granthi*. Some of them join in the singing. People make offerings to charity, just as they do when they worship at home. They will all join in the *langar* meal, which is provided for free to anyone visiting the temple. Twice an hour, 3,000 people eat a *langar* meal. This also shows that all Sikhs are equal because everyone shares the meal, regardless of status. Some people may then choose to bathe or wash in the holy lake around the temple.

Bandha's story

"My name is Bandha and I am ten years old. I live in Ireland with my grandparents, mother, father, and twin brothers. I am going to go to Amritsar this April. I am so excited because I am going to meet lots of other Sikhs from all over the world. But most of all I am looking forward to sharing the *langar* meal with thousands of people. We will all feel equal, special, and very proud to be Sikh."

Pilgrims place flowers on the floor of the Golden Temple. ▶

Festival pilgrimages

There is no set time when Sikhs should go to visit these special sites, but Sikhs often go at festival times such as Baisakhi, Diwali, the birthdays of Guru Nanak and Guru Gobind Singh, or the martyrdoms of Guru Arjan Dev and Guru Tegh Bahadus. Baisakhi is the busiest time to go, as it is the main festival. At this time, Sikhs remember the founding of the *Khalsa* by Guru Gobind Singh. On Baisakhi day, the Guru Gobind Singh asked the faithful to be prepared to lay down their lives for their faith. At Baisakhi many choose to be baptized into the faith and wear the Five Ks, the symbols of Sikhism (*Kara*—a steel bracelet; *Kirpan*—a small dagger; *Kesh*—uncut hair; *Kangha*—a comb and *Kachera*—shorts), to show that they too are Sikhs.

Going on journeys to the holy sites is very enjoyable and is a very special time for Sikhs. It gives them the chance to share their experiences with people from all over the world and celebrate their beliefs together. It is also a private time when some choose to refresh their faith and remember the values of equality and justice that are so important to their religion.

GLOSSARY

Abraham (or Ibrahim), the prophet who taught Muslims not to worship idols.

Adam the first man, created by God.

Baisakhi (BUY-sock-ee) the Sikh festival that remembers the founding of the *Khalsa*.

chanting rhythmic and prayerful singing.

chastity refraining from sexual activity, often for religious reasons.

cremation the burning of the human body after death.

crucifixion the Roman method of execution by nailing the victim to a wooden cross and letting him or her die.

deities gods or goddesses.

disciples the first twelve followers of Jesus.

Diwali (duh-VAHL-ee) a festival celebrated by Sikhs to remember the release from prison of their sixth *Guru*, Guru Gobind Singh. It is also celebrated as a New Year festival by Hindus.

Enlightenment a state of freedom from pain and suffering.

Five Pillars of Islam the religious and moral duties of a Muslim.

granthi a Sikh leader who reads from the *Guru Granth Sahib*.

gurdwara (GOORD-wuh-rah) a Sikh temple.

guru (GOO-roo) one of the 10 Sikh human teacher-saints. Name given to a Buddhist teacher who is Enlightened.

Guru Granth Sahib the Sikh holy book.

Guru Nanak the founder of Sikhism.

Hajj (HODGE) the Islamic pilgrimage to Mecca.

Hasidic (hah-SID-ick) a very strict and pious form of Judaism, which started in the 18th century in Europe.

Holocaust the extermination of six million Jews by Nazi followers in the late 1930s and early 1940s.

Khalsa (KAHL-suh) the Sikh community.

Koran the Muslim holy book.

Krishna the Hindu god Vishnu became Krishna when he came to Earth to overcome evil.

langar a shared meal that is eaten in a Sikh *gurdwara*.

martyr someone who is killed for his or her beliefs or faith.

Mecca the Muslim holy city in Saudi Arabia.

meditation to concentrate on an image or a sound to clear one's mind or to think good thoughts.

monastery a religious community of monks and or nuns who live together.

Muhammad the most important prophet in Islam.

Passover (Pesach) (PAY-sock) a festival remembering the Israelites' escape from Egypt.

Persecution the ill-treatment of a group of people because of their beliefs, views or practices.

Satan the angel who was thrown out of heaven for sinning and became the enemy of God.

Shavuot (SHUH-voo-ut) the Jewish festival remembering the revelation of the holy texts, the *Torah*, on Mount Sinai.

shrine a holy place

stupas (STOO-puhs) burial mounds containing important Buddhist relics.

Sukkot (SUCK-ut) Jewish harvest festival.

Virgin Mary Jesus' mother.

Wesak "Buddha day," the festival that remembers the birth, Enlightenment, and death of the Buddha.

Zamzam a sacred well in Mecca.

FURTHER INFORMATION

Books

Chambers, Catherine. *Sikh* (Beliefs and Cultures). Danbury, CT: Children's Press, 1997.

Ganeri, Anita. *Buddhist* (Beliefs and Cultures). Danbury, CT: Children's Press, 1997.

Goldman, Alex J. *I Am a Holocaust Torah*. Hewlett, NY: Gefen, 2000.

Hunter, Elrose. *The Story Atlas of the Bible*. Parsippany, NJ: Silver Burdett Press, 1996.

Kenley, Karyn. *My Favorite Bible Stories* (The Beginner's Bible). New York: Little Moorings, 1995.

Penney, Sue. *Judaism*. Austin, TX: Raintree Steck-Vaughn, 1997.

——. *Sikhism*. Austin, TX: Raintree Steck-Vaughn, 1997.

Quinn, Daniel P. *I Am Buddhist*. New York: Rosen Group, 1996.

Rock, Lois. *The Time of Jesus*. Colorado Springs, CO: Lion Children's Books, 1999.

Wood, Angela. *Buddhist Temple*. Milwaukee, WI: Gareth Stevens, 2000.

——. *Hindu Mandir*. Milwaukee, WI: Gareth Stevens, 2000.

GENERAL SERIES ON RELIGION:
Beliefs and Cultures series (Children's Press, 1996–1997)
Discovering Religions series (Raintree Steck-Vaughn, 1997.)

Websites

http://www.sikhfoundation.org/ – The Sikh Foundation
http://www.hindusamajtemple.org/ht/hindu.html – An introduction to Hinduism
http://www.islamicity.org/ – An introduction to the world of Islam
http://conline.net/ – Christians Online, a Christian resource
http://www.jewishweb.com/ – The worldwide Jewish Web

INDEX

All the numbers in **bold** refer to photographs